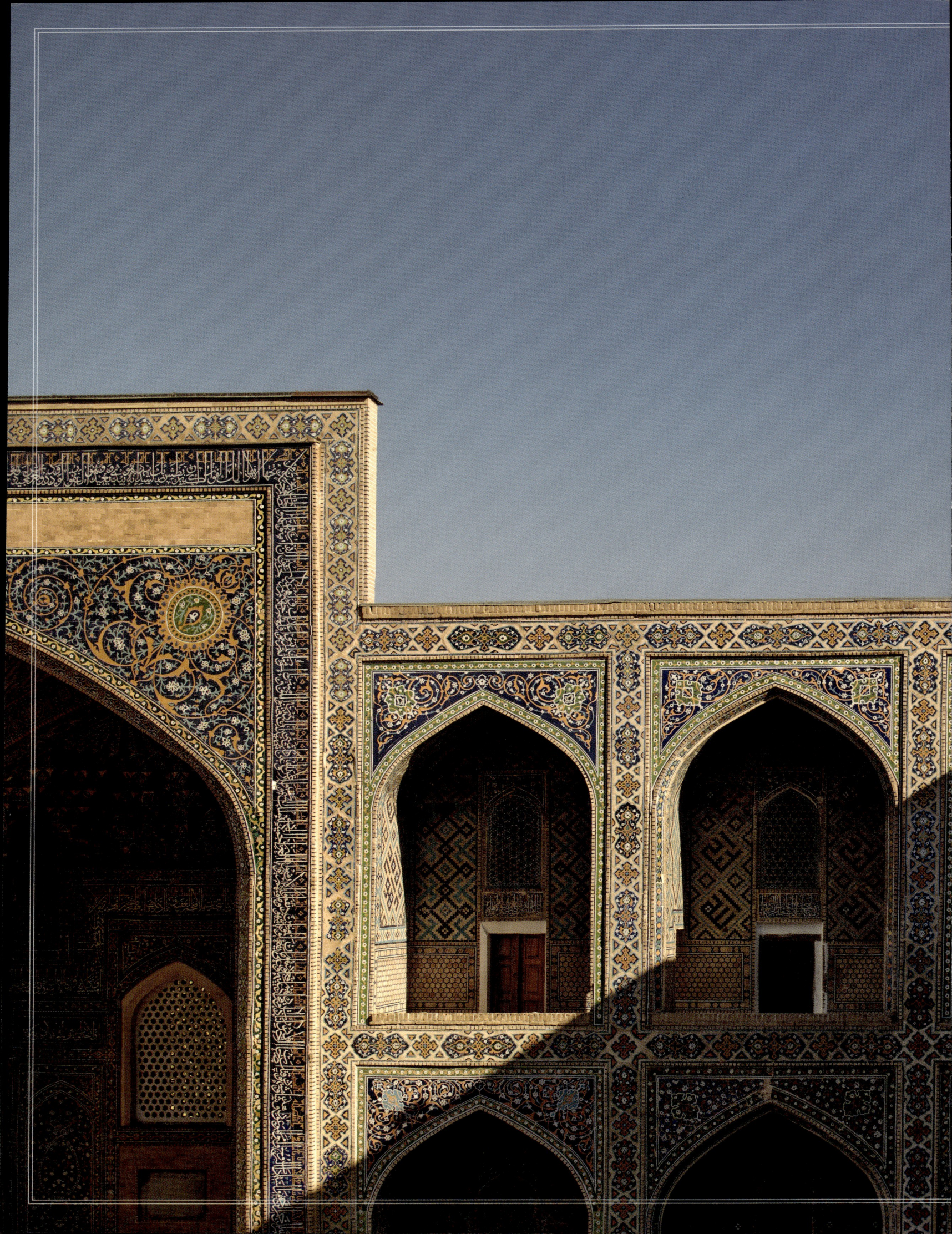

CABANA

CABANA ANTHOLOGY

THE ANNIVERSARY EDITION

crafted by

**MARTINA MONDADORI
CHRISTOPH RADL
MIGUEL FLORES-VIANNA
BARBARA SPINELLI
GIULIA BISCOTTINI
CAMILLA FRANCES
LAETITIA ALFANO**

TABLE OF CONTENTS

p. 23
FOREWORD
by Deeda Blair

p. 25
HAPPY BIRTHDAY, CABANA!
by Martina Mondadori

p. 27
I GOT YOU BABE
by Christoph Radl

p. 28
A HOUSE OF MAGIC

p. 44
ELECTRIFYING ARCHITECTURE

p. 56
THE STEFANIA MANSION

p. 72
INSIDE - OUTSIDE

p. 88
DISCOVERING LISBON

p. 104
FINDING TIME

p. 116
UMBERTO PASTI: MY WAYS

p. 118
BLESSED BY GODS

p. 134
THE STYLISH SUBVERSIONS OF PORTALUPPI

p. 150
IN THE PINK

p. 166
PHARAOHLAND

p. 182
THE FREEDOM OF CREATIVITY

p. 196
THE QUEEN'S HOUSE

p. 208
TRANSYLVANIA

p. 226
HARMONIOUS SIMPLICITY

p. 238
AN UNEQUALLED ARCHITECTURE

p. 252
CABANA COVERS

p. 254
THE VIEW FROM VISTORTA

p. 270
WYETHS' WORLD

p. 286
A LOVE OF THE FRAGMENT

p. 302
THE PROMENADE OF DONNA ENRICHETTA

p. 318
VIENNESE DELIGHT

p. 334
IN THE MIND'S EYE

p. 352
VELYAN'S HOUSE

p. 366
KING FOR A NIGHT

p. 374
OUTRAGEOUS FORTUNE

p. 390
WANGDUECHHOELING PALACE

p. 402
THE ONCE AND FUTURE CASTLE

p. 422
ACKNOWLEDGEMENTS

p. 424
CREDITS

Foreword

by Deeda Blair

When the first issue of *Cabana* appeared on newsstands, it had an instant impact. Its curiosity and the quality of its imagination felt entirely new: possessed of a vibrant, adventurous spirit, *Cabana* could take hold of you and lend you its energy in astonishing ways. I had never read a magazine like it, nor have I since.

Perhaps that is because Martina Mondadori, Christoph Radl, and their talented team have created something far beyond a magazine; they have united a global community of people with immense curiosity who explore and collect examples of unforgettable beauty. They have redefined how we look at interiors, gardens, and architecture. Through *Cabana*'s disruptive, distinct, and uncompromising pursuit of creative excellence, they have travelled to all corners of the globe, visiting places we could never have expected to discover for ourselves. In matchless prose, enhanced by peerless photography, *Cabana* is written with the precision and personality of a memoir. In every issue, you can trust that the editors will reveal something beautiful, rarely thought of or experienced, and give it the care and attention it has long been due.

This Anniversary Edition weaves together some of the most remarkable places explored and shared by *Cabana* over the last decade. It will take you to Malta for a tour of the Queen's House: the now-abandoned residence where, unbeknown to many, the late Queen Elizabeth II enjoyed several happy years. You will discover the beautiful, contemplative estate of Cy Twombly at Bassano in Teverina, and the magnificent home of the Brandolini d'Adda family in Vistorta, Italy. Always it is a great pleasure to read *Cabana* a second or third time.

You will be inspired and delighted by the pages that follow. They are full of imagination, freedom, and independence, and *Cabana* always dazzles with exceptional pictures and the infinite possibilities of memorable creativity. Diverse architectures, lost antiquities, libraries, power plants, walls of wisteria, meadows, gardens, the weaving of a pattern, and the budding of a single flower: each is considered individually but all are linked by their frame, the distinctive borders that edge these pages. Turn them, and you will find yourself tracing connections of your own.

Happy Birthday, Cabana!
by Martina Mondadori

It was April 2014 when our first issue of *Cabana* came out. In the grand scheme of things, ten years is not such a long time. But in a modern society where all is speed and change, the world now feels quite different from the one we knew back then.

Cabana was born into a fertile landscape. There was an appetite for something fresh, a hunger for an aesthetic that championed atmosphere over function. Perhaps the social and economic instability that characterised the years after 9/11—the wars and financial crises that we are still, sadly, witnessing today—nurtured a certain longing for cosy interiors and vintage fashions. In uncertain times, we turn to comfort food and the past for reassurance; maybe we were a warm croissant on our readers' cold and rainy days.

Of course, this is easy to say in retrospect. Back then, it felt simpler. There was a flash of intuition, and we trusted it: we planted a seed in the right soil and at the right time. With care and attention, it grew and flourished. *Cabana* is the story of like-minded people coming together and sharing their passion and vision with the world.

What has driven this passion? The spirit of discovery is at the very heart of this project. That's something our ever-growing community of contributors, readers, and subscribers all have in common. We all love discovering these layered, soulful interiors and their delightfully eccentric inhabitants, exploring distinctive cultures, and searching the past and present for exquisite objects and textiles.

Often, people ask me what makes an interior right for *Cabana*. I always have a simple answer—quality and originality. That is harder to achieve than it sounds because, as the best designers know, balancing a space is a delicate task. There is always a strange alchemy at work in the homes we feature, and we are passionate advocates for the artists and creatives who weave their magic in such places.

Our armchair travelling has taken us all around the globe and through centuries of history. We want to continue to take these journeys, the flights of fancy where dreams are born. As I write this piece, I am thinking of our next decade, excited to embrace whatever changes it may hold. Let's keep our antennae switched on, ready to sense the next flash of inspiration.

I Got You Babe

by Christoph Radl

Looking back has never been one of my favourite pastimes. I tend to forget about my projects the moment the ink is dry. But now, as I flip through the pages of this Anniversary Edition, which collects the best features from *Cabana*'s first decade, I am struck by a curious sense of déjà vu—and in my mind, I swear I can hear a song begin to play: "I Got You Babe," by Sonny & Cher, a memorable motif in the movie *Groundhog Day*.

In the film, Bill Murray's character, Phil Connors, is trapped in a time loop, condemned to wake up each and every morning to that same single song, "I Got You Babe." When he realises what is happening to him, he starts to take risks to break the spell: he gets drunk, he despairs, he fights, he gives up, he even attempts suicide. But there's nothing to be done about it. The next morning, the same day starts again, and the same song is playing on the radio. Phil doesn't know it yet, but only love can liberate him.

With *Cabana*, something similar happens. Each time we prepare to work on a new issue, it feels as though we are reliving that first day all over again. Ten years ago, we decided to try to open a new page in the world of interiors. We contacted friends, photographers, authors, interior designers, gardeners, intellectuals, journalists, and lovers of beauty who could give us advice, contacts, ideas—anything. And between discussions, layout tests, and text corrections, a small group of people worked incredibly hard to make our vision for *Cabana* a reality.

One day, we woke up, and there it was—our first issue. A fabric cover concealed a thousand beautiful surprises, our dreams spread out on fine and glossy pages. Ten years have passed, but every six months there still comes the day when a new issue of *Cabana* arrives. Always the same and always different, nothing can compare to the surprise and joy that comes with watching a new and wonderful world unfold before your eyes. Our family grows, the discussions intensify, ideas emerge faster and faster, image quality improves, the number of pages increases, and over time we have become braver, more extroverted, and more refined. We take risks. We get drunk on patterns. We fall in love with colours, with poor and simple things, with richly elaborate artisanal styles, and in this whirlwind, the idea of transporting the visual culture and the aesthetic mood of *Cabana* from the two-dimensionality of the page into the world of objects emerged with more and more insistence. So, we broke the spell. We bundled together all our emotions, inspirations, and aesthetics, and began to explore the three-dimensional world, choosing the table as a playground. Today, we make products of real artisanal quality: plates produced with Richard Ginori, glasses blown and hand-painted in Murano, placemats braided in South America, ceramics from southern Italy, Tuscan napkins embroidered by patient hands, and many other beautiful things.

I could not have imagined all this ten years ago. What might the next decade hold?

Cabana—I got you babe. And you got me.

A House of Magic

Words by Susana Ordovás
Images by Brett Wood

It is a typically hot and humid morning in Mérida when I arrive at Xuna'an Kab for the first time. I take note of the imposing facade, typical of the old houses along the Camino Real, and spy unruly vegetation peeking over its tall and austere walls. I suspect I am in for a treat.

Bruce Bananto, the former New York interior designer, welcomes me into the heart of Xuna'an Kab. We arrive in a grand space, a foyer and dining room that branches out to the rest of the house. Mysterious murals adorn the walls, my eyes linger on their strange and beautiful patterns.

Bananto settled in Yucatán in 2015, drawn to the region by its temperate climate and rich architectural history. When he first saw Xuna'an Kab, he knew he'd found what he'd been looking for. "I wanted to rebuild it and give it another century of life. It was missing its ceilings and giant tropical trees grew inside, but it had such an exquisite bone structure. I didn't want this house to be renovated by someone who didn't love it—it would lose its soul." The unusual motifs on the walls were inspired by the ceiba tree, known to the Maya as *ya'axche*, "The Tree of Life." For them, the ceiba links three worlds: the base of the tree is a part of our world, the world of men; from there, its roots stretch down into Xibalbá, the underworld, while its trunk reaches up toward the heavens. Its branches are said to be the dwellings of the gods and the entrance to paradise. Bananto painted each by hand himself, using only traditional materials—paints of chalk and milk, tempera, and wax.

I venture through the rest of the house, where blue, green, and lilac play counterpoint to warm shades of grey and beige. The limestone walls, always damp in Yucatán, age a painted finish almost immediately, creating an extraordinary patina. The architectural elements and the furniture are masculine, with a dash of whimsy. There is an eclectic mix of styles, melding Tuscan, Moorish, and ecclesiastical influences, all threaded throughout with references to the natural world. "We are face to face with wild animals and tropical plants every day inside this city. I wanted to paint what I was experiencing," Bananto says.

The local stoneworkers were the first to call the house Xuna'an Kab, naming it after the stingless honeybee native to the surrounding rainforest. The Maya consider these bees sacred, believing them to be descendants of the gods themselves. I stand on the porch, taking in the house for the last time. Xuna'an Kab is a fitting for name for this magical place, so lovingly restored, and I feel certain that its soul has been preserved for centuries to come.

Electrifying Architecture

Words by Cosmo Brockway
Images by Mark Luscombe-Whyte

Jules Verne once said, "Well, I feel that we should always put a little art into what we do. It's better that way." Once the primary source of electricity for the city, Budapest's Kelenföld Power Station is a testament to this idea. When its Art Deco design was first unveiled in 1914, the power plant was hailed as a wonder of its age, praised for its harmony of form and function, its sweeping scale, and its grand visual style. Architects Kálmán Reichl and Virgil Borbíró had built a utilitarian jewel.

The government decommissioned the station in 2007, as it neared a century of service. Under Hungarian law, Kelenföld can neither be destroyed nor ever resurrected. But for the faint rustle of the trees outside, today it stands in silence, frozen and sealed beside the Danube like the tomb of a nameless pharaoh. Magnetic, desolate, and eerily beautiful, it has not lost the genius loci that made it a marvel to those who knew it first.

The control room at its heart is especially entrancing. The banks of buttons, gauges, and dials are arranged in concert, like sections of a strange orchestra, one that could hear music in the hum of current. Light leads the eye up to an ornate stained-glass ceiling, a sumptuous addition from 1927 that echoes the design of the era's cruise ships. It bestows the room with style and grandeur—along with a touch of pathos—and leaves visitors with an image of Kelenföld as a pale green *Wunderkammer*, sinking into the murk of time. Below the stained-glass ceiling and to one side of the control room sits a small concrete bunker, happy and anomalous, designed in the style of a sentry's hut. It offered workers shelter from Soviet bombers in World War II —thankfully, it never needed to be put to use.

Standing in the quiet of this vast space, watching the play of light and shadow, it is hard to imagine that this was the first electricity supplier for the region and Europe's earliest electricity exchange. Those functions have no more part in its destiny. Nature will overtake this place, and, with time, nothing will be left of it—but until then, there will be glimmers of human life here. The space, already beloved by filmmakers, will become even more lyrical and cinematic, and countless new artists, architects, and writers will come and discover these chambers for themselves, for if there was ever poetry in architecture, it was written here, in Kelenföld's industrial stanzas.

The Stefania Mansion

Words by Sofka Zinovieff
Images by Miguel Flores-Vianna

When you reach the Stefania Mansion House, the door's knocker is shaped like a lady's hand. Grasp it. Turn the key. Inside, all is quiet, perfumed by jasmine, polished wood, a hint of amber. Or is it frankincense, wafting up from the nearby convent? Patmos is a religious place, and its devotion to beauty always possesses a spiritual dimension. These homes are themselves the relics and reliquaries of merchants and treasure-hunters—but history can wait till the morning. Up the stone staircase and inside the cool bedroom, there are fresh sheets, soft pillows.

I wake to sunshine and spectacular views: across the fields to the chapel-topped mountain, and over the old town all the way to the Icarian Gulf. Back inside and down the stairs, a terracotta-coloured kitchen boasts a 400-year-old carved-stone wellhead and a functioning underground cistern. I switch on the electric light to confirm I woke up in the right century, but I needn't have worried—all the mod cons are present and correct, tidied away into kitchen cupboards. I take breakfast in the "secret" garden among the apricot and lemon trees, while outrageous sprays of bougainvillea dash white-washed walls with pink.

My hosts arrive, and we go upstairs for coffee in the sala. Although the furnishings look like they've been there forever, the wood-framed sofas, floor cushions, and giant brass tray table are arranged for contemporary life. Gilt mirrors hang angled away from the walls, resting on narrow wooden ledges in the Patmian style. Muted colours reflect elegant restraint: the walls are white, the floorboards bare, the shutters and doors painted sage and dove grey.

The house dates to the early seventeenth century, but its owners did not want to live in a museum—they wanted to create a home that was authentic but alive. Over the years, antique beds, sofas, hand-crocheted blankets, and wooden chests were acquired locally or from neighbouring islands, and the owners did not limit themselves to the Aegean, sourcing the huge rug from Florence, the bathroom curtains from Cairo. Two portraits of a nineteenth-century couple turn out to be Maltese. Their eclecticism is appropriate, for this is what prosperous Patmians have done for centuries—combine Levantine aesthetics with touches of the European, the Russian, and the Eastern: Samos ceramics and Venetian glassware; Parisian fashions and home-spun blankets; local goats' cheese and Oriental spices.

Before leaving on the midnight boat, I watch the sunset from the bedroom that faces the Aegean. The sea darkens to purple, and a rosy light tints the doves that swoop and circle over Zoodochos Pigi, the Convent of the Life-Giving Spring.

Inside-Outside

Words by Cosmo Brockway
Images by Mark Luscombe-Whyte

On the shores of Lake Dudhwa lies the hidden demesne of one of Sri Lanka's most enigmatic figures, the late architect Geoffrey Bawa. Born in 1919 to a Burgher family of mixed descent—he had Sinhalese, Scottish, French, and German heritage—he went to England to study law at Cambridge and architecture in London before returning to Sri Lanka, where, on a whim, he bought the old rubber plantation Lunuganga. A French cousin had suggested he might earn a living by his obvious talent for creating spaces. "I have plenty of money," was his reply over tea, to which his relation, Georgette Camille—friend of Picasso and Braque—said, "I have much more money than you, and I can tell you it runs out."

Like the sculptor who sees his form inside the block of marble, Bawa chiselled away and brought forth his own Eden at Lunuganga. His original plans are marked by a forensic level of detail, right down to the individual leaves on the surrounding trees. During construction, he would use a megaphone so he could continue directing work while he sat and took his afternoon tea. His first act—relished by the locals, who appreciate eccentricity—was to clear away perfectly good rubber trees to open up a view across the lake to the distant hilltop stupa of Kalutara.

"He brought modernism to Sri Lanka, but he deftly translated it for the island. He accepted our history and environment and wove them into a fresh story," says Channa Daswatte, chair of the Geoffrey Bawa Trust. On the slope of land he called Cinnamon Hill, Bawa placed a Ming urn under an old Moonamal tree, using a relic of the old Portuguese spice trade as an eye-catcher. Bawa wanted to cultivate a sense of the "inside-outside" here. Wandering past pavilions and through garden rooms, visitors find elements of English Romanticism, the Oriental, and antiquity brought together in strange and happy consonance. The loggias are nestled between sculptural frangipanis, classical statues brought from Italy are speckled with lichen and moss, and giant palm fronds, with shadows like those of prehistoric birds, dapple the sunlight streaming through the windows. On the south lawn stands a brick gazebo, where the man himself would sit on clearer nights, hoping to "catch a glimpse of centaurs in the pineapple fields."

Years ago, a group of Japanese visitors were so impressed by the golden patina of the Sandela Pavilion that they had to ask the architect its age. "Oh, about six weeks," came his airy reply. The force of Bawa's imagination was such that it seemed able to bend time and space in service of his aesthetic vision. "Geoffrey was a master at inventing a story out of nothing," says Daswatte, "and nowhere is this clearer than at Lunuganga."

Discovering Lisbon

Words by Carlos Mota
Images by Mark Luscombe-Whyte

While exploring Lisbon, you can visit Portugal's most magnificent palaces and churches. However, you should be cautious, because with every twist and turn, you may unravel a hidden gem, and it's possible that a charming *rua* or a picturesque square will steal your heart along the way. When *Cabana* offered me the opportunity to work on a story here, I was delighted—I've fallen for the thief, and Lisbon is quickly becoming my second home.

Our photoshoot took place on a rainy Sunday, and I found myself in what seemed like a hidden corner of Lisbon—a place with an air of mystery and adventure. I walked into the courtyard, and I took in Palácio do Grilo for the first time. This place has a long history, stretching back to the start of the eighteenth century. It was badly shaken by the Great Earthquake of 1755, and repairs and renovations went on throughout the nineteenth century. Now it stood before me, a little weathered, perhaps, but undeniably graceful. It wears its history proudly, and there is a certain elegance in its endurance.

The palace evokes the grandeur of the largest residences of Italy or Russia but on a smaller scale—a more intimate marvel, achieved with greater economy. Having been all over the world, I can confidently say that the oculus room stands as one of the most impeccably designed spaces I have ever encountered. It is a masterclass in proportion and scale, and every fresco and detail add to its charm. Opening onto the garden, it offers two atmospheres: closed doors create an intimate and cosy space, perfect for winter; flung open, it transforms into a fresh and happy summer room.

I like to dream of the events that might have taken place here, imagining the vibrant scenes: the parties, the balls, and the captivating romances that graced a life at court. This being an eighteenth-century palace, with its own chapel and chinoiserie room, one has all the settings one would need to stage a drama, and with a touch of history, characters too begin to emerge—figures like Duke Pedro Henrique de Bragança, at one time the owner of this palace, the half-brother of the king of Portugal, and a key player in the dance of politics and influence.

Finding Time

Words by Nicholas Cullinan
Images by François Halard

In the spring of 1972, Cy Twombly bought a dilapidated house at Bassano in Teverina, in the countryside north of Rome. Spending three years working on the restoration, he turned Bassano into his country residence and summer studio. Cradled in surrounding woodland, the house was quiet and isolated, and a far remove from the urban clamour of Twombly's Roman apartment. Bassano's peaceful atmosphere would come to have a profound influence on his work.

"I like bucolic poetry," Twombly said, "Theocritus, Virgil. When I used to spend time in Bassano, you could still see shepherds tending flocks of goats. Once I actually saw one throw himself down under a tree and play a flute." With *The Shepheardes Calender* (1977), Twombly consciously embraced the pastoral tradition, taking Edmund Spenser's poem for his title and his own surroundings as his subject, using subtle gradations of shade and colour to trace the shifting of the seasons at Bassano.

Inside the house, the mood is hushed and contemplative. Certain collections of Twombly's photographs figure his studio as a muse —and behind these immense stone walls, it's clear that these monumental interiors influenced some of his most major work. The polyptych *Fifty Days at Iliam* (1978) was painted here, in three different rooms over the course of two summers. As art historian Kirk Varnedoe suggests, the "decor of fragmentary Roman sculptures... the tapestries of military conquest... [made] a propitious setting for a rumination on Hector and Priam."

In the '80s, Twombly continued to experiment with natural themes inspired by the surrounding landscape. *Untitled (Bassano in Teverina)* (1985) is part of the series of "green paintings" that dominated his output in this period. In these paintings, Twombly worked en plein air, striving to capture the fugitive effects of light as it dissolved into shadow over the forest outside his studio.

The last major series of works that Twombly made here were two sets of the *Quattro Stagioni*, begun in July 1993 and completed at his seaside house in Gaeta. These are meditations on the cyclical patterns of nature, the changing of the seasons, on shifts of light and the passage of time. The sun-bleached canvasses for Summer owe much to the Gaeta house, but the sombre mood and sylvan themes in Autumn speak only of Bassano. Two of the variations relate to Bassano's wine festival and its bacchanal origins—for Twombly, life here still follows the twin rhythms of nature and myth. As he said of Bassano, "It still lives here, that Mediterranean world. And nothing that's living is old to me."

Umberto Pasti

my ways

What a whirlwind of a man! Umberto Pasti is such a rich mix of traits and talents that he's nearly impossible to portray. A writer, collector, horticulturist, historian, garden maker, and philanthropist, he is also an aesthete who is intuitive, discerning, curious, practical, poetic, earthy, and filled with wonder. He is at once very grown-up-worldly and very childlike. (Bonus: He's funny, too.)

If an in-person encounter isn't in the cards, I think the best way to get to know Umberto is to read one of his seven books and then take a deep dive into the hundreds of photos online and on paper depicting his three residences. There's a house in Milan, a villa and garden in Tangier, and a house and large property in Rohuna, about forty minutes south of Tangier, where Umberto has funded and mobilised an entire rural Moroccan village to grow and tend to gardens, make rustic furniture, and produce folklorique objects and toys to support themselves.

Whether urban or rural, Umberto's homes tell countless stories from many lands and many centuries: there is nothing gratuitous, frou-frou, or show-off-blingy in Umberto's rooms. There are fine pieces and lots of "beloved neglected things." To be sure, it's all maximal. Still, every Islamic tile, Neolithic kilim, Berber ceramic, Roman bowl, Indian textile, Greek sculpture, Spanish painting, North African basket, Neapolitan table, whalebone, and jumbo shell is highly prized, loaded with good background stories, and often perfect in its imperfection. An Umberto Pasti house is a giant *cabinet de curiosités* with a PhD in world history, beauty, and sentiment.

His assemblages are deliciously heart- and mind-felt.

In fact, if Umberto were inclined to take up interior design—and he is *Definitely Not* so inclined—he would be one of the greatest decorators of all time. But as it happens, Umberto Pasti is so much better off living as an artist who paints with words, plants, objects, friends, neighbours, and a charming partner who cannot be duplicated. His life is indeed his art.

Marian McEvoy

Stone tools from the Paleolithic to the Neolithic, Roman marbles, old fabrics, Moroccan painted furniture, Islamic pottery, African art,

Ottoman ferns bulbs, seeds, masks Neoromantic drawings by lits of carpets, 18th century furniture... bulk tiles, and begonias, books, Berber toys, from New Guinea, paintings, Philippe Jullian, classical "poor" painted But the of my

COLLECTIONS is the first one, that I started as a kid: the feather headresses from the Americas, Africa, Borneo. I still love them even if I never know where to wear them.

The Moroccan shelf (morfa) watches benevolently over the few Italian BOOKS

That I keep in my studio in Tangier, the only ones in my library that are not in order.

A bowindow in our place in TANGIER that I copied from old houses in Cairo and Fez. How many times I rang the bells of those apartments and asked the tenants stupefied if I could take some measurements!

I could spend days to find a proper name for each of the reds in this picture. As it

happens with everything, a COLOUR exists only if it has a name.

Why to call TRAVEL a quiet corner of a sitting room, which evokes reading or sleeping by the fire? Because the Ottoman carpet fragment comes from a sale in Germany, the little lamp from a junkshop in Bretagne, the two white pots from the Tunisian Pau in the the Spanish ones from in Lisbon, Madrid, the Moroccan from and Tétuan...
And I the long on the

Puglie, tiles from Pyrenées, and Portuguese dealers Sevilla, Toledo, tables Clignancourt remember trip Rif mountains under the snow, the village where I found one of the painted jewellery boxes in the garage where the owner was fixing my car.

This NOW ON THE OCEAN furniture made in Rohuna is the only thing I'm proud of. Few families live thank to it.

For this I feel like a rooster.

ROHUNA for me is a garden, but when inside

the house I spend most of the time in the kitchen.

THE TALE OF MANY TALES
is introduced by a Venetian chap
that drives away the evil eye 👁

Then a long story begins...

STEPHAN is Stephan Janson, my
angel,  he is
not a Moroccan
table. But if
I blow his secret
name in the
shell that a muezzin
was using to call
the faithfuls to the
prayer, sometimes
he comes.

I'm very lucky.

I would love the all world to be

BEGONIALAND!

Blessed by Gods

Images and Words by
Miguel Flores-Vianna

The sky above Denizli was golden as our plane approached the airport. Some years ago, I had read in *Cornucopia* magazine about the distinctive mosques in the villages near this Turkish city, a vibrant centre of textiles lying at the foot of the Taurus Mountains. Dating from the eighteenth and nineteenth centuries, they are characterised by naive floral patterns painted in an extraordinary variety of vivid colours.

Now, I was on my way to photograph them. Looking from my window, I saw the gold disc of the sun obscured by drifting nimbus clouds, airy and immense. Only twelve hours ago, I had left London under a grey slab of sky—now, high above Eastern Anatolia, amidst clouds softly rounded like the domes of the mosques below, and I felt like I was soaring through fireworks.

The mosques were one or two hours' drive from one another, dispersed among small villages in the foothills of the mountains. For three days my friend and I drove through forests of oak and pine, listening to Erik Satie, Miles Davis and '70s Turkish pop on the radio. We took in the countryside, stopping by lakes for fresh fish and in valleys to eat fruit from fragrant orchards.

At each mosque, new friends brewed us cups of tea and served handfuls of nuts and dried mulberries. Inside, we noticed the buildings shared characteristics besides their floral patterns. All of them were inscribed with verses of the Koran, and their ceilings were often decorated with geometric designs. At times, we would visit when they were empty, but their walls always seemed to hold the echo of the morning's chants and prayers. The effect was impressive, but not in the lofty manner of the Hagia Sophia or Süleymaniye Mosque—these holy places possessed a humility and warmth that is hard to achieve at a grander scale.

Each mosque made a strong visual impression, but we'd also leave with human stories. At Belenardıç, the delicate voice of the old mullah was as dazzling as the turquoise paints he showed us, and at Hirka, the *masjid* was a confection of pink, pistachio, and blue—its delightful palette in perfect sympathy with the happy sounds of the wedding lunch held in the garden that afternoon. At Akköy Mosque, when a group of little girls joined us to practice their English, I found the way their giggles and colourful garments filled the room every bit as beautiful as the bloom of the thousand flowers painted on the walls.

The Stylish Subversions of Portaluppi

Words by Nicolò Castellini Baldissera
Images by Guido Taroni

My great-grandfather, the architect Piero Portaluppi (1888-1967), knew Milan to be a city of secrets. He sensed that her subtle allure could not bear too much disclosure. As Italy's productive capital and counterweight to Rome, the Milanese sensibility eschews the decadence of the Eternal City, so, Portaluppi subverted the grandeur of the *palazzo* for the charm of the *palazzina*. For him, the beauty of Milan needed to be gradually discovered—it could not be overtly revealed.

Portaluppi was born in 1888 and graduated from the Politecnico di Milano in 1910. He received his first major commissions from his future father-in-law, Ettore Conti, in 1913. Conti, in the process of electrifying northern Italy, asked the young architect to design several hydroelectric power plants—some of which still stand today. In these early works, there is a visible play between a sweeping, grand modernism and his deep attention to decorative detail that delineates the private and public and communicates each space's function. Like most of Portaluppi's work, all of the properties featured here were built for the haute bourgeoisie (including, eventually, himself). What we see here is a small collection of the architect's work around the midpoint of his career, a time when his neoclassical references were humorous and rationalism had not yet dominated decoration. At Casa Corbellini-Wassermann, recently restored and reopened by the gallerist Massimo De Carlo, slabs of marble are laid like ribbon candy, leading visitors through the space. At Casa degli Atellani, the hand-laid mosaic floors mirror the wave-like pattern of the front gate. Strips of glass, chrome, and bronze are woven within the various doors, walls, and ceilings of his buildings. Tartan appears everywhere, from the radiator covers to the terrazzo pavement. Growing up on the top floor of Casa Portaluppi, every day I passed a little house, the symbol of his studio, tucked in by the staircase of the ground floor (which today houses the Fondazione Portaluppi). This is a perfect example of his rich sense of humour. It comes as no surprise that Portaluppi's first job was as a cartoonist.

His daring buildings stand out with their unusual geometries and stylistic repetitions, and look particularly modernist from afar. But closer inspection reveals decorative flourishes recalling Baroque Italy. Portaluppi's inventive use of materials—intricate marble designs, wrought-iron gates, mahogany doors, brass radiator covers, and even simple handrails—provided a new architectural vocabulary for Italian urbanism. It was rich, forward looking, and unchained from the aristocratic establishment.

In the Pink

Words by Charlotte di Carcaci
Images by Tim Walker

My grandmother Barbara Cartland was born in the stolid Midlands, a robustly handsome brown-haired girl who would transform herself into a glorious anomaly. She bleached and teased her hair until it resembled spun sugar, fluttered her long false lashes under turquoise eyeshadow, and wore spectacular chiffon gowns that dripped with jewels, feathers, sequins, and diamanté. She became a glittering confection of extravagance.

So it was with her house, the sturdy Italianate mansion built in 1867, with an interior suited to heavy upholstery, antimacassars, and jungles of indoor palms. Under the spell of Barbara's imagination, it was transformed into a candy-coloured Xanadu. Although she bought the property in the '50s, its decorative style harks back to the '20s, when the tomb of Tutankhamun was first discovered and Egypt was all the rage.

Starting out as a young journalist in London, Barbara made an immediate impression on high society. She found a mentor in Lord Beaverbrook, one of the great press barons of the period, and by the time she became engaged to the heir of a publishing fortune—my grandfather, Alexander McCorquodale—she had already declined forty-nine proposals for marriage. As a young wife and mother, Barbara threw lavish costume balls, inviting the beauties of the day to dress up to a given theme. To her "Superstitions" gala, Barbara went as the Spirit of Good Fortune, wearing a headdress in the shape of an enormous silver horseshoe, a satin gown embroidered with four-leaf clovers, and a black cat perched on her arm.

It was in these years that she began writing her novels. In the photographs from that time, she is ever the young authoress, gazing pensively into the middle distance with a pen in her hand. She wrote bestseller after bestseller and brought a boundless energy to everything she did. At one point, she could produce a new book every fortnight and still find time to tirelessly advocate for the causes she believed in, be they the loan of dresses for war-time brides, or the establishment of "Barbaraville," a permanent encampment for Romani travellers.

While we were photographing the house, each room a riot of vivid silks and gilded furniture, we discussed what exactly constitutes the quality of camp. My grandmother's style was always flamboyant, but it was never ironic—and I believe that for something to be truly camp, it must have a sense of irony. In the same way that the heroine in a musical finds it impossible to convey emotion with words alone and must let her feelings soar into song, Barbara could not be contained by the strictures of conventional decor. Here in this house, in all this brilliant excess, her romantic sensibility still finds its full expression.

Pharaohland

Images by Miguel Flores-Vianna

Soon after joining Christie's in 1967, I was assigned a small cubbyhole in the office of Tony Derham, one of their experts in Chinese art. We became firm friends, and remained so for many years thereafter. From this small patch of territory I was instructed to build up "The Department of Islamic Art," the geographical context of which stretched from Spain to China. It was the first time an auction house had had such a thing. A while after my arrival, Tony was promoted to auctioneer. On the morning of his first sale as such, while he perused the catalogue to familiarise himself with the reserve prices, registered bids, and so on, we were interrupted by the arrival of a smartly dressed, blazer-clad gentleman, an elegant Levantine, who engaged us in lively conversation. When it was time to go down for the auction, Tony asked me to accompany Mr. B and look after him. We stood at the back and watched the proceedings, conducted with crisp efficiency by the new auctioneer. Halfway through the sale the star item was put on the block: an unusually large early Ming blue-and-white dish. It made a world-record price, not much by today's standards, but then a great sum, meriting a mention in next day's *Times*. At this point Mr. B put his hand on my arm, steered me out of the rooms and downstairs to the lobby. "That Ming dish was mine," he told me, "I bought it in Cairo for £5. Please join me for lunch at the Ritz at 1 o'clock, I have things to discuss with you."

Over lunch he explained that he had long before befriended an Armenian family who owned a big villa in Cairo, and who had collected over generations all sorts of Islamic art. It was a subject Mr. B knew little about. The family was forced to leave Cairo when Nasser came to power, surrendering their considerable business interests. The villa, however, remained legally theirs. It was boarded up and had become invisible, looked after by an elderly relative who inhabited what had been the servants' quarters. In order to boost his meagre pension, this relative was prepared to sell works of art from the villa, but only to people designated by his cousins in exile. The curious thing, said Mr. B, is that everything, whatever it is, is for sale for the same price: £5. Including the Ming dish that had just sold. He then described what he had seen but didn't understand, particularly the values thereof. Chests of Ottoman velvets, Mamluk enamelled glass, carved wood and stone, ceramics, paintings, and so on. Assuming that I knew about such things, he asked if I would be prepared to join him in Cairo the next time he went. A couple of days later I made an appointment with the managing director of Christie's, told him the story, and suggested that here was an extraordinary possibility to boost the profile of the market for Islamic art. There was a long pause, until he looked up at me with undisguised hostility. "You are forbidden to go to Egypt for any purpose, or under any pretext." Three weeks later, on a Monday morning, a telegram arrived from Mr. B: "arriving Cairo Thursday stop send flight details stop will meet you at airport stop." At lunchtime I walked to the office of Syrian Arab Airlines off

Continues on page [181]

off Piccadilly, which provided the cheapest fares for the Middle East, and bought a ticket to Cairo scheduled to arrive in the evening of Thursday. Before leaving for the airport I called Christie's to say I was ill, and found myself embarrassed by the sympathy offered in response to my fraudulent illness. Mr. B was clearly as much at home in Cairo as in other capitals of the world, and took me from the airport on a whirlwind tour of the social life of the city. At each stop we seemed to accumulate more people in our train, until we ended up in a belly-dancing establishment on the road to the pyramids. Dawn streaked the sky by the time we left, and there was little time to sleep since an early start was scheduled for our visit to the villa. Mr. B had not exaggerated the interest of what lay concealed there. In room after room we opened cupboard after cupboard and chest after chest, while he questioned me about each piece extracted from its yellowing newspaper wrapping: its origin, its age, and above all its possible value. Not everything was of interest, but the good things, and there were many, reflected a refined connoisseurship. It took most of the day to complete our investigation, and finally in the late afternoon I wandered out into the courtyard to breathe some air free of dust. There I saw, under the portico, a great jumble of architectural elements, the wooden pieces stacked upright against the back wall and the stones strewn over the floor. As I was pulling out a wood panel to get a better look at it, the elderly guardian shuffled over to my side. "That comes from Ibn Tulun, you know, the frieze beneath the ceiling." I hadn't expected such expertise from a man who, up until that point, had seemed to be tethered to this world only by the weight of the jelaba that enveloped him. We proceeded around the portico and he gave me a history lesson on the Islamic buildings of Cairo as illustrated by the fragments before us. It was in one corner of the portico I spotted this slab of porphyry. "That was part of an imperial Roman building here, and later re-used in an early fourteenth-century mosque," my new professor explained. Forty years before, he went on, most of the great Islamic buildings in the city were in a state of dereliction. When bits fell down they were left where they lay. The buildings became quarries of stones for new buildings in the local quarter, and the wood, as often as not, was gathered by the poorest classes and used as firewood. I supposed he was right about the porphyry slab. Mining began in the Gebel Dokhan mountain under the Ptolemies in the third century BC, and was abandoned in the fifth century AD when the cost of the huge infrastructure involved could no longer be sustained. From Tiberius's time onwards, all porphyry belonged exclusively to the emperor. After mining ceased, the porphyry used to embellish later Byzantine and Islamic monuments was recycled from the buildings of the Roman Empire.

When I informed Mr. B of my wish to buy the slab he looked doubtful. Small pieces were easy to transport, he said, but large items were more problematic, and particularly because I wanted to keep the slab, it was a lot of effort for no profit. Eventually we agreed that it would be sent separately at my risk. I didn't mind how long it took, and anyway £5 was not such a grave risk. It was indeed many months later that I was summoned to Tilbury Docks to clear it through customs, and the ride home in a taxi cost more than the slab.

With business done in Cairo, Mr. B decided it was time to move on to Beirut, where there were more things to show me. That Saturday night I eluded his grasp and was taken by friends to a restaurant in the Bekaa Valley. It remains a vivid memory because it was the first time I had seen at each place on each table a Lucky Strike packet containing twenty neatly rolled joints. When I arrived at Christie's on Monday morning, after four near-sleepless nights, no one doubted I had suffered a nasty bout of flu.

From "Red Porphyry Slab," in Every Object Tells a Story *by Oliver Hoare, London, 2015*

The Freedom of Creativity

Words by Cosmo Brockway
Images by Guido Taroni

Perhaps only Idarica Gazzoni could pack up a palazzo like a Bedouin moving her tent. Wanting to be closer to her showroom—she is the founder of cult textile brand Arjumand's World—she dismantled her home in Rossini's palace in Bologna and decamped to an eighteenth-century former *casa di ringhiera* in Milan. Idarica took down her waterfalls of ikat silks, folded up the Anglo-Indian daybed, and cut up a vast Persian rug so she could install them in her new rooms.

She had been seduced by the first apartment she looked at. "By chance, I knew it well. It belonged to my old friend Raimonda Lanza. I used to spend many happy evenings here, surrounded by curated treasures and much laughter." The designer was taken in afresh by its balanced proportions, its sense of history. "The wooden beams… the curve of the rooms, wending along the old Via Santa Marta… the echo of traditional life from the balcony. Speaking my name that low-lit afternoon, I felt as though I made it mine."

Idarica painted the bone-white salon a cerulean sky-blue and veiled the bookcases with bamboo chik blinds. Above the marble fireplace, a striking velvet *Haiti* is framed by Egyptian ceramics glazed in Faiyum. While most of the furniture has been re-covered in white cotton, two low slipper chairs are upholstered in Kink of Pearls, a fabric of Idarica's own design. "I chose white because I wanted a feeling of clarity, of polish," she laughs. "When possessions follow you around, they can feel weighted. To change their appearance is a small act of escape." Dancing shadows lead the eye into the dining room beyond. Here, the space is flanked by antique mirrors, and rows of Ginori flowered china bloom against walls of hessian-gold. Above, there hangs an oversized crystal chandelier—a Lanza design, inspired by the baroque interiors of the Palazzo Reale di Torino. "I have placed its pair in my bedroom so I can lie and watch the reflections play," Idarica says, leading me to her bedchamber. The Uzbeki fabrics lining the walls are kept loose, billowing like folds in a courtesan's gown. "Here are two things I would never leave behind," Idarica says, "the tiny oil painting of a sleepwalking figure, a gift from my mother… and the iron campaign daybed, given to me twenty-five years ago. It reminds me of great female explorers like Jeanne Baret and Lady Hester Stanhope." No stranger to travel herself, Idarica had recently returned from the frescoed mansions of India's Shekhawati desert. "It was so inspiring… those murals depicting the lives of caravan-laden merchants, painted in the most extraordinary colours."

Idarica's Milanese warren is as magnificent as any palazzo. If you have the space to dream, you have all the room in the world.

The Queen's House

Words by Ashley Hicks
Images by Miguel Flores-Vianna

This is Villa Guardamangia, the house where the late Queen Elizabeth II and Prince Philip lived in Malta in 1950-51. They first arrived as guests of Philip's uncle, my grandfather, and made it their home when he left the island. It was here at Villa Guardamangia that the young wife of a junior naval officer had a brief taste of "normal life," before her father's untimely death put a crown upon her head. With her epic reign now ended, the villa's empty rooms are possessed of a new poignancy.

My family's connection with Malta began in 1869, when my great-grandfather Prince Louis of Battenberg arrived aboard the HMS *Ariadne* as a fifteen-year-old midshipman in the Royal Navy. In 1887, he returned as Commander of HMS *Dreadnought*, joined there by his daughter, Alice—who would one day be Prince Philip's mother—and his wife Victoria. At the time of her engagement, her namesake and grandmother Queen Victoria had written to her that the "only drawback I see… is 'the fortune.' I don't think *riches* make happiness, but I do think a certain amount is a necessity." It was true that Louis and Victoria were far from having a fortune—but their younger son Louis, known as Dickie, was sensible enough to marry into one. Dickie and the heiress Edwina Ashley were my grandparents, and their home in Malta, just across the street from Villa Guardamangia, was the luxurious Casa Medina. In the '30s, they lived here in great style, with beds from Heal's, a yacht in the harbour, and Dickie's polo ponies stabled at nearby Marsa.

After the war, they returned to the island in 1948. They had served as the last viceroy and vicereine of India, living in a palace with a staff of over 500, and adjusting to a more normal life in Malta was not easy. Edwina wrote to her beloved Jawaharlal Nehru that "one feels one's brain and even one's energy shrinking to fit the tiny island." They rented Villa Guardamangia and had it completely redecorated, Edwina still scouring the island for lamps and furniture at Christmas. Later, Dickie wrote to thank her for "the best decorating job of your life," but besides the dolphin doorknocker and the eau de Nil tiled bathroom, sadly little of her work remains.

Prince Philip arrived as first lieutenant of HMS *Chequers* in October 1949, and Princess Elizabeth joined him a month later. Edwina gave them her bedroom and moved into Dickie's, leaving him a guest room. She told Nehru that with all the royal staff that it felt like "Piccadilly Circus," but that it was "lovely seeing [Elizabeth] so radiant and leading a more or less normal and human existence for once." When the couple left, Edwina wrote to Nehru that "putting her into the Viking [airplane] was like putting a bird back into a very small cage and I felt sad and nearly tearful myself."

Transylvania

Words by **William Blacker**
Images by **Mark Cropper**

When I first travelled to Transylvania in 1990, I expected to find a country populated by a bewildered, downtrodden people emerging blinking from the darkness of forty years of Communist conformity. In the late '80s, the dictator Ceaușescu had planned to "systematise" the villages, to bulldoze traditional houses and move their inhabitants into apartment blocks—making it easier for him to control the masses.

What I found there was the precise opposite. Western newspapers had been at pains to paint the gloomiest of pictures, but it seemed that barely any "systematisation" had occurred. The villages I travelled through were intact and unspoiled, brimming with cheerful and fresh-faced people of all ages. They wore brightly coloured traditional clothes; some, setting off for work in the fields, carried scythes, wooden hay rakes, and hay forks on their shoulders. Pear-shaped hayricks decorated the hillside, and the houses below were washed in bright colours: blues, ochres, greens, and pinks, their eaves boasting fretted decoration interwoven by the climbing vines. It was where I had come from that seemed drab and grey. Sometimes, I felt as if I were travelling more in time than space, through a rural, medieval world brought to life from the pages of some illuminated manuscript.

In 1996, I returned to live here, immersing myself in a different way of life. Old wooden looms took up half the kitchen in the winter, when village girls and women would weave textiles for their homes and for the church. At Eastertime, the girls would promenade in their fine new smocks, adorned with delicate embroidery. Their attire, fit for queens of old, was made as intricately as possible to demonstrate a girl's skill and industry, with a view to attracting a suitor. The villagers made all their own hats, baskets, and shoes; when I needed a belt, an old man made me one in fifteen minutes using dried animal pelt, beating out a buckle from a few odd pieces of metal on a small anvil. One day, Mihai, the man in whose house I lived, was sitting in the courtyard making hay rakes. I saw that he was cutting a design into the head of the rakes, notching out small sections in between the tines. I complimented him on the trouble he took to make his tools beautiful. "No, Willy," Mihai said, "it is to make the rakes lighter."

This straightforward, gentle way of life had survived Communism, and until only recently, continued to fill Romania's villages with objects of a pure and functional beauty. Nowadays, this timeless world is fading. Villagers must emigrate for work and mass-produced consumer goods are commonplace. Many houses have already been abandoned, and the winds of change blow through empty rooms that were once filled with so much colour and laughter.

Harmonious Simplicity

Words by Natasha A. Fraser
Images by Miguel Flores-Vianna

Last July, Edouard Vermeulen celebrated forty years of designing Natan Couture. Based in Brussels, the sixty-seven-year-old Vermeulen is the favourite couturier of Northern European royalty. At weddings, abdications, and all the most important ceremonies of state, whole courts of queens and princesses trust Vermeulen to dress them. The glamorous Máxima of the Netherlands, her predecessor, Beatrix, and Mathilde of Belgium have all worn Natan for many years, trusting that this silver fox is sensitive to their needs. Appreciating that his clients are under fervent scrutiny, he takes a subtle approach. He's fond of the occasional feather, but a Vermeulen cut flatters and enhances—it doesn't shout or overwhelm.

Vermeulen's second home is in Knokke-le-Zoute, a charming seaside town about an hour's drive from Brussels. Zoute has attracted its share of artists, including Dalí, Magritte, and Man Ray, Niki de Saint Phalle and Jean Tinguely, but it remains a traditional, family-oriented place. Instead of buying a house, Vermeulen acquired a plot of land in the heart of town. Working with the architect Stéphane Boens, a childhood friend, the house took eight months to build—"I was sixty-one years old and not at all rushed: very *piano, piano*," he says. Although he was inspired by the '50s and the Flemish architect Viérin—"particularly his work in Bruges"—Vermeulen wanted his new thatched-roof home to look as "if it had always been there." He needed the weekend residence to function in both the winter and summer months and be "large enough for entertaining, but not too large when alone."

Keeping a close eye on the project, Vermeulen "was able to change" certain aspects of the design as it developed. He dislikes the warrens of bedrooms that are a feature of Zoute's oldest Anglo-Norman houses—"at my age, it just wasn't an option"—so he established three guest suites on the first floor to create "the most comfortable conditions," joining two smaller bedrooms on the second floor with a shared bathroom. "I was rigorous about the dimensions of the rooms, the distribution of light and was eager to make the perspectives as long as possible." Along with the enfilades, Vermeulen thought "an entrance hall with double-height ceilings and a sculptural staircase that felt timeless" would match the house's minimalist and airy spirit. The goal was authentic simplicity—oak floors and white walls throughout, using paint "as white and natural as possible—no synthetics." Apart from the burgundy-coloured canvas on the staircase, everything else was purchased for the house. He worked with interior decorator Jean-Philippe Demeyer ("he places everything beautifully") to put sculptures by Sterling Ruby and Florian Tomballe into harmonious arrangement with beautiful ceramics to bring in "colour and texture."

An Unequalled Architecture

Words by Anuradha S. Naik
Images by Mark Luscombe-Whyte

"When the moon was in the constellation of Leo and Jupiter was in his own mansion, Sultan Quli Qutub Shah ordered architects and masons to prepare the plans of a city, unequalled the world over and a replica of paradise itself." (Firishta, 1560–1620)

The fifth sultan of the Qutub Shahi dynasty, Muhammad Quli, founded the city of Hyderabad in 1591. He laid it on a grid with a central square and ordered the construction of shops, schools, mosques, caravanserais, and baths; when everything was ready, his court moved into the new city. Hyderabad was an extension of the fortified capital Golconda, which had become too small for its burgeoning population. By then, Golconda was synonymous with luxury; the world's only known diamond mines were some of its holdings.

Today, Golconda still stands, albeit in ruins and subsumed by the city that grew out of it. From the fort's high ramparts, the majestic vista now includes the monumental tombs of Hyderabad's founders, the Qutub Shahi. They hailed from Iran, but these sultans imbibed and assimilated local traditions, and their architecture reflected this syncretism. Cusped Indian arches were decorated with ceramic tiles, and large colourful domes had lotus motifs at their bases. Under the shah, Hyderabad became a kaleidoscope of oriental splendour and a hub for the trade of pearls, diamonds, ivory, steel, silk, and printed cotton. It was a vibrant, cosmopolitan, and thriving city, replete with Persian, Arabian, Armenian, Dutch, English, French, and Portuguese traders.

The Charminar occupies the centre of the original grid and dominates the old city of Hyderabad. Not just an ornamental gateway, it was used as a mosque, a school, and a place to make proclamations—and it even served as the headquarters of the French army under Marquis de Bussy-Castelnau in the eighteenth century. From 1687 Hyderabad was briefly occupied by the Mughals, until a viceroy of the emperor declared its independence in 1724 and established a new rule under the Asaf Jahi Nizams.

Over the course of the nineteenth century, the British East India Company grew in power and the British Residency became a second node of authority. As Hyderabad incorporated more European influence, the skyline changed dramatically—but until the turn of the twentieth century, it was not uncommon to see Hyderabadi nobles, mounted on gorgeously caparisoned horses and surrounded by armed guards, wend their way along the narrow streets, trying to avoid the trample of the elephants carrying Hyderabadi boys to school.

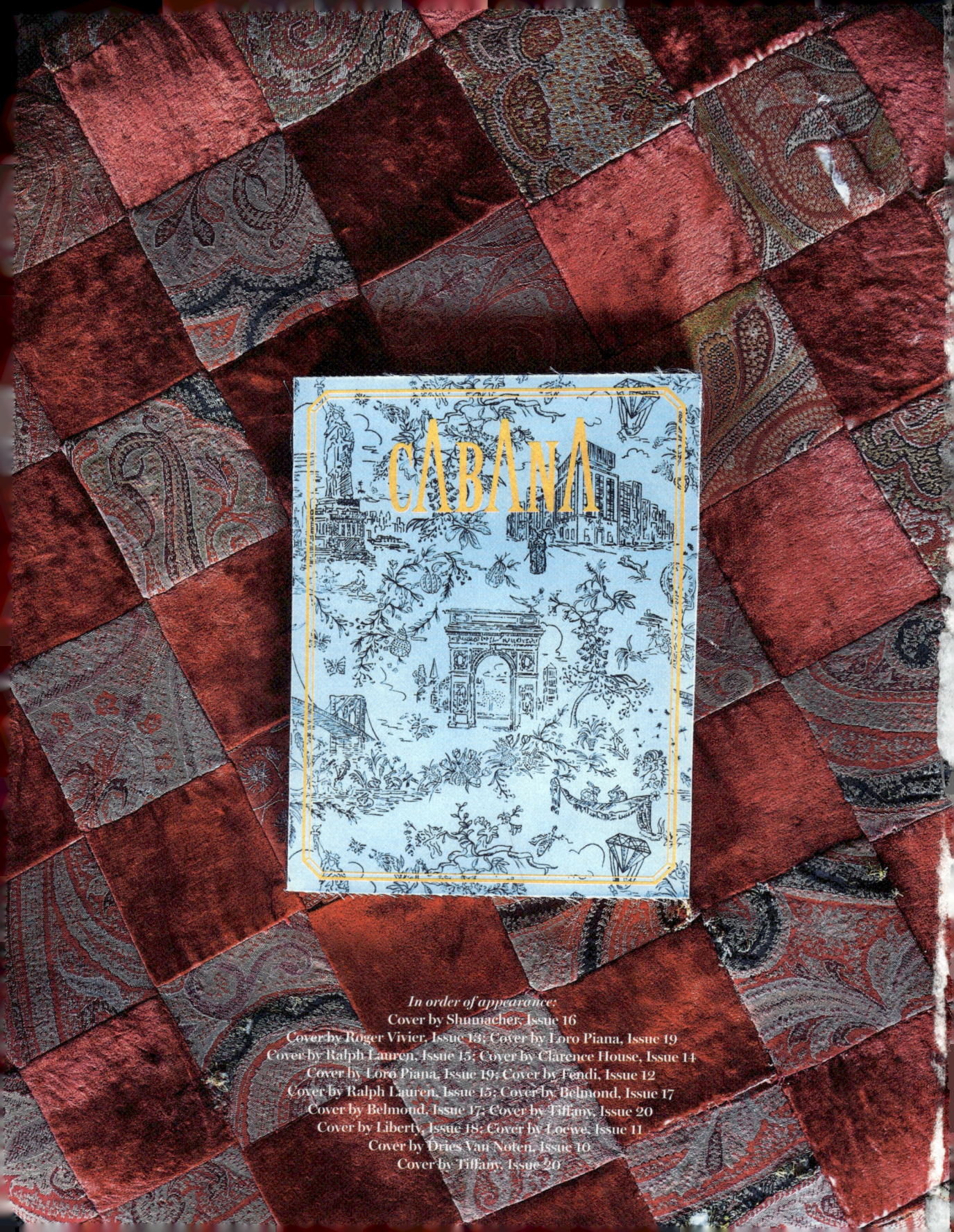

In order of appearance:
Cover by Shumacher, Issue 16
Cover by Roger Vivier, Issue 13; Cover by Loro Piana, Issue 19
Cover by Ralph Lauren, Issue 15; Cover by Clarence House, Issue 14
Cover by Loro Piana, Issue 19; Cover by Fendi, Issue 12
Cover by Ralph Lauren, Issue 15; Cover by Belmond, Issue 17
Cover by Belmond, Issue 17; Cover by Tiffany, Issue 20
Cover by Liberty, Issue 18; Cover by Loewe, Issue 11
Cover by Dries Van Noten, Issue 10
Cover by Tiffany, Issue 20

The View from Vistorta

Words by Natasha A. Fraser
Images by Miguel Flores-Vianna

Before her marriage in 1947, the nineteen-year-old Countess Cristiana Brandolini d'Adda was given a choice. Either she could live in the family's sumptuous Palazzo on Venice's Grand Canal, or she could retire to Vistorta, a dilapidated nineteenth-century villa set on a 500-acre estate in Veneto. The adventurous art student opted for the latter. "Built by my husband's Great-Uncle Guido, Vistorta hadn't been lived in for thirty years, but I recognised that it was a place of great charm," says the now ninety-six-year-old matriarch. To achieve Vistorta's full potential, "it had to be a big family house—but not boring and traditional," she says. For the renovation, the countess approached the relatively unknown Renzo Mongiardino, who would go on to become one of the most sought-after architects and decorators of his generation. "He immediately said, 'We have to make it less bourgeois.' That was his main goal," she says; Mongiardino wanted a "Russian house," like those in the novels of Turgenev, Chekhov, and Pushkin.

The architect and his client may have had their creative differences—"since Mongiardino had a bad temper, I changed things behind his back," Cristiana admits with an impish laugh—but the house is considered one of his masterpieces. The seamless line-up of frames, the opulent drapery, the innovative paintwork, and the appliqué woodwork on the doors are all unmistakably Mongiardino. In some ways, it feels more authentic than much of his later work, despite Vistorta being his first important commission. "It's weathered well," agrees Cornelia "Coco" Brandolini, Cristiana's oldest grandchild. For Coco, Vistorta is a nostalgic place. "My earliest memory is of my grandfather Brando listening to opera," says the forty-five-year-old designer. "The house was shaking with Maria Callas. I went downstairs and found him sitting alone in the salon, looking a little teary-eyed and emotional." She remembers how the count would take her around the park, teaching her the names of plants and animals. "Both my grandparents were very touched by the beauty and force of nature," she says.

In the summer months, the Brandolini brood adjourns to the terrace after dinner, to sit on the stone steps and look up at the stars. This is a special place for each generation of this tight-knit family—and their shared memories of Vistorta continue to bring them closer together. For Coco, her grandmother remains her "biggest inspiration," she says. "As someone who's met everyone and seen it all, she never criticises the younger generation. Open-minded, she always sees something interesting." Her grandmother feels their bond just as strongly. "I get smaller and smaller with age, but Coco always takes me in her arms," says Cristiana, smiling. "Her love feels important."

Wyeths' World

Words by Remy Renzullo
Images by Ari Kellerman

Compared to the trite, clichéd images so often identified with coastal New England, Andrew Wyeth portrayed a different sort of Maine, and in doing so, may have shaped his audience's perception of a place more than any other contemporary artist. His was a darkly romantic vision of a vanishing agrarian world, and the architecture of rural America was fundamental to it.

His homes share in the austere nostalgia of his art, but they owe a lot to the influence and efforts of his wife and collaborator, Betsy James. Allen and Benner, a pair of rugged islands six miles off the Maine coast, were a canvas for both their talents and their summer home. Previously the domain of local fisherman and their families, Betsy saw a quiet beauty in the clapboard buildings that dotted the coastlines. Supplementing these with new structures of her own design, she created waterfront villages to serve as homes and studios for the couple. Each building has a specific purpose—library, studio, kitchen— and demonstrates an easy fluency with the local vernacular. When sparingly used, simple folk-art pieces like hooked rugs, slipware, and sailor's valentines become tremendously elevated and aesthetic decorations. Southern Island, a five-minute sail away, is crowned by a whitewashed lighthouse purchased by Betsy in 1978 that passed to their son Jamie Wyeth in the '90s. Jamie—also an artist—eschews his parents' sparsity in favour of a more layered approach. A seasoned collector, he knows what he likes and what he's looking at, but as wonderful as the pieces are, his unpretentious arrangements ensure his rooms have warm and companionable atmospheres. His house here, set within the decommissioned nineteenth-century lighthouse, is a world suspended somewhere between the past and the present, grounded in the simple beauty of the ordinary—characteristic of Jamie's own deeply moving work.

Further out from shore lies Monhegan Island, the last bit of land before the vast openness of the Atlantic Ocean. The furthest house from the village is the Rockwell Kent house, so named for its former owner, another legendary American painter. This is a stunning example of Maine's twentieth-century coastal design: painted floors, slipcovered furniture, and walls hung with narwhal tusks and a whale's jawbone. Upstairs, shells encrust the architraves and ceiling of an attic bedroom, a dazzling evolution of the dozens of sailor's valentines arranged downstairs.

American artists have defined the Maine aesthetic, and no family has contributed more to this than the Wyeths. Maine is their vision, their world; their homes are the embodiment of their art, and their art is the embodiment of this special place.

A Love of the Fragment

Words by Marco Mansi
Images by Antonio Monfreda

Born in 1906, Carlo Scarpa is undoubtedly among the twentieth-century architects who most successfully explored the expressive potential of light. For almost his entire life, he lived in Venice, the city of water, beauty, and light; and it was always a Venetian light that illuminated Scarpa's work, be it reflected by the marble walls of a palazzo or scattered on the surface of a glittering canal.

He reached artistic maturity swiftly and with little apparent effort. As Stefan Buzás has noted, Scarpa's early projects already show the emergence of a system of shapes, colours, and materials that would make his style inimitable. By the end of the nineteenth century, architectural approaches had diverged, with some favouring structure, others ornamentation—but Scarpa sought to reconcile the two, at both a practical and intellectual level.

For Scarpa, beauty was the common denominator; ornamentation makes architecture attractive by enriching it with meaning. In his work, every fragment is a unit imbued with significance—the detail and the whole have equal value. The architect used materials in such a way as to enhance their sensory characteristics and intrinsic decorative properties. The transparency of glass, the graininess of concrete, the warmth of exotic wood, and the deep sedimentation of Aurisina stone allowed him to create new dialogues. Scarpa liked to employ ancient techniques and skills in his work, but he was always without nostalgia—he never forgot that he wanted to make something new. "Those who ask you to imitate window styles forget that they are the product of other materials, styles, and ways of creating windows… and such imitations always turn out to be tawdry," he warned.

His work on museums and exhibition spaces marks the high point of his creative endeavours and earned him international acclaim. Scarpa translated his pictorial sensitivity into the spaces he designed, filling them with light and the refined play of colour and material. When we look at famous sculptures and paintings in these spaces, we have the feeling we are looking at them for the first time. Bruno Zevi was right to call Scarpa's designs "formal lyrical events." In the sparing, essential quality of all his projects, each fragment is brought into a perfect whole by craftsmanship, experimentalism, and close attention to the contemporary. This photographic portfolio aims to capture the enigmatic, revelatory magic wrought by the man Kurt W. Forster once called the "shaman architect."

The Promenade of Donna Enrichetta

Words by **Umberto Pasti**
Images by **Guido Taroni**

From the moment my dear friends shared with me the photographs of this palazzo in Calabria, and told me of a certain Donna Enrichetta—who, borne on the shoulders of her servants, collected tithes from tenant farmers while still seated in her sedan—there's been nothing to be done about it: I simply cannot get her out of my head. I know I've never seen her, not even in a portrait, but she seems to materialise before my eyes: sallow skin, a grim mouth with the whisper of a moustache; slight in build, reclining in a sedan like a little waxen saint beneath a dome of glass. She is smiling, but the peasant girl has scattered too much grain. She draws the curtain, calculating. How many barrels will that vineyard yield? How many quintals from that olive grove? What catch will come from the sea today? Will that scoundrel Pippo finally get around to—"My bones! Do you want to break them, wretches?" she scolds the saddle-men. She calls on Santa Rita, makes the sign of the cross, and blows a kiss to baby Jesus, while the four fellows sweat up the rocky path.

As I admire the interiors of the estate, I wonder why my beloved Donna bequeathed it to the Sisters of Reparation as an orphanage. There must have been conditions; Donna would have been very firm. When the Bishop came to call, he met only the most adorable children, mouths full of marzipan, chubby thighs pinched to a healthy glow by the nuns. The others, having emptied the chamber pots, had only to do some laundry, a spell of weeding in the vegetable garden, and scrub the Caltagirone floors before they earned the privilege of spending the rest of the day on their knees in the chapel, and then perhaps they could have some scraps to eat. *Tictictictic...* All is shattered by a quick-fire WhatsApp. My informer does something that should never be done with an Italian journalist—furnish him with verified information with which to write an article. No, Donna Enrichetta was a wonderful woman, a generous philanthropist: she had churches built, she bestowed dowries on needy maidens, she repaired an aqueduct to quench the thirst of her neighbours. And the Sisters of Reparation? They were heroes, religious and kind! I cannot conceal my disappointment. Just then, my Donna Enrichetta was alighting from her sedan, riding crop in hand, her heel sunk into the calloused palm of a bowing porter. The scent of the sea, the murmur of the mulberry trees in the wind, the crickets, the crescent moon... What next, my Donna Enrichetta? I'm no longer certain. Is it my fault if southern Italy is still a land of abuse and injustice, trimmed all in lace? It has always been this way.

My Donna: she is Calabria, through and through.

Viennese Delight

***Words by* Michael Huey**
***Images by* Miguel Flores-Vianna**

When Lady Mary Wortley Montagu passed through Austria in late summer 1716, the poet marvelled at the height of buildings in Vienna. At the time, it was a walled city, so the only way to expand was up. She was also shocked at how fast and recklessly carriages careered through its narrow streets. Vienna is no town of quick fashions, and in these two matters, it remains virtually unchanged. It is not uncommon for motorists to intentionally accelerate toward languid jaywalkers—not to actually hit them, of course, but just enough so that the ensuing drama of braking hard and laying on the horn may unfold—and the city's architecture remains about seven stories high.

Today, this has a rather different effect to the one Lady Mary experienced. The scale of nineteenth- and early twentieth-century structures seem small-town, the taller buildings still genuflecting to church spires. Looking out from the Gloriette, a hilltop folly at Schönbrunn, one sees steeples poking through the fabric of the cityscape like little thorns and burrs on clothing. From that same spot, one can peer into the windows of the palace below, where the aged widow Maria Theresa once sought to escape from the summer's heat. In 1769 she commissioned Bohemian painter Johann Baptist Wenzel Bergl, known for his loose and open brushwork, to paint the rooms with exotic landscape scenes in an "Indian, American, or Japanese" manner, while her son and co-regent Joseph prepared his political reforms. A ten-minute walk from Bergl's rooms takes us via 130 years of Austrian design, from Rococo to Secessionism, to Wagner's Hofpavillon: the royal station on the city's early light-rail line, built in 1899 for Maria Theresa's great-great-grandson, Emperor Franz Joseph I. From here, the rest of Austria's twentieth-century architecture and design is visible on the horizon. Wagner had trained with Theophil von Hansen, architect of the Austrian Parliament, the other key Ringstrasse buildings nearby. He employed Jože Plecnik in his atelier, and his students included Joseph Maria Olbrich, who designed the Secession Building, and Josef Hoffmann. Wagner and Hoffmann carried over ideas about privacy from the era of Maria Theresa, and their aesthetic influences were Josephinian neoclassical and the pure, tectonic forms of Austrian Biedermeier. Like the German language, Viennese high style was long a unifying factor among the different nationalities of the Habsburg realm, before culture wars and nationalistic identity politics began to prevail at the turn of the century.

Austria's aesthetic tradition is long and persistent, even if most Austrians today often feel it more in their gut than in their consciousness. Lovers of the ambiguous, they seem to prefer it this way. Not infrequently, the results are sublime.

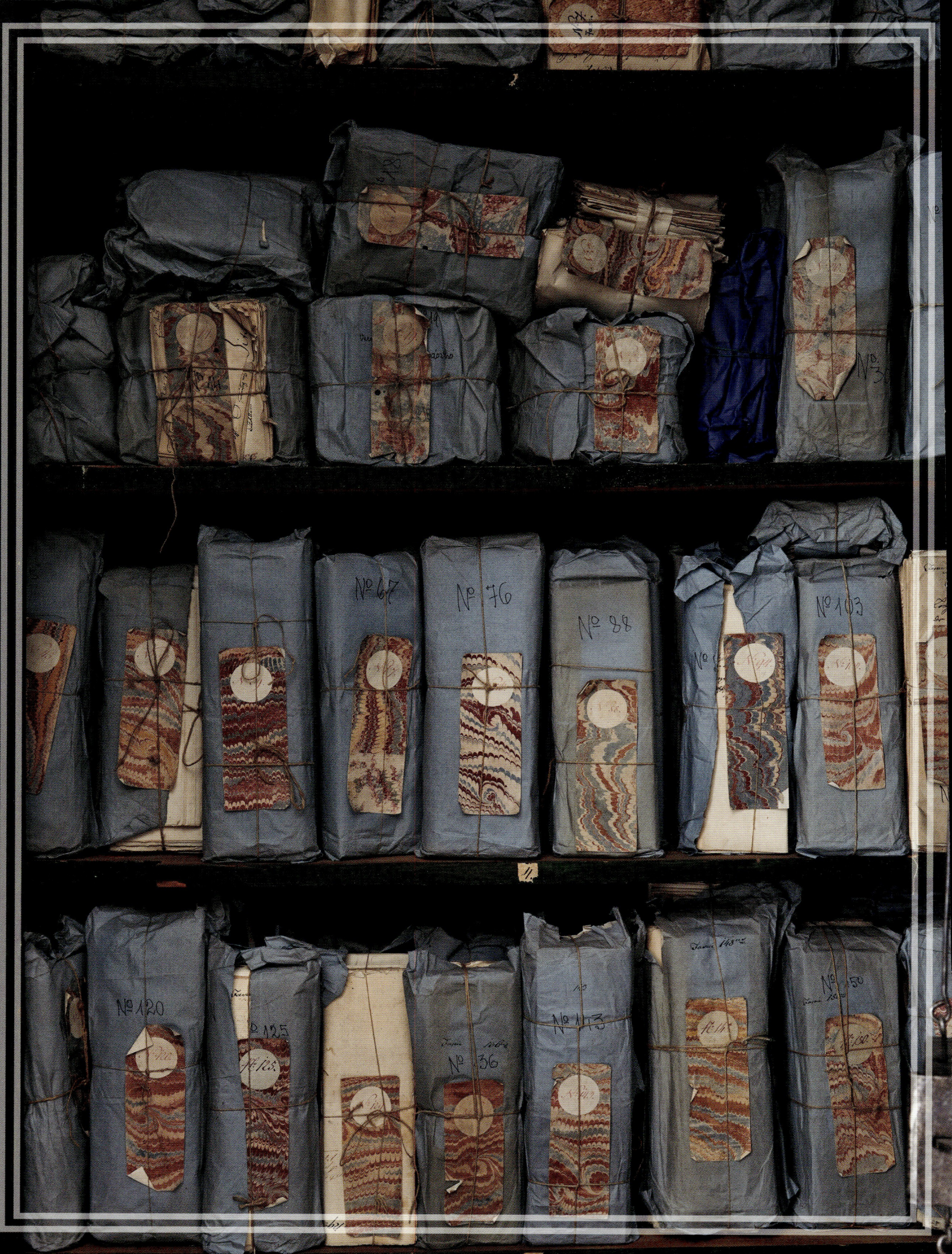

In the Mind's Eye

Images and Words by
Miguel Flores-Vianna

In January of 2011, I spent ten days in Syria. I had long wanted to visit the country, not only for its vast repository of the remains of ancient civilisations, but also because it was still relatively cut off from the rest of world. I wanted to travel *à l'ancienne*, to throw away my smartphone, to follow the advice of friends, well-thumbed books, and my own nose. I wanted an adventure.

I arrived in a quiet and wintry Damascus on the evening of January 2nd, to meet my friend Sandra Nunnerley, who had decided to join me on my trip. That first night at our hotel, I confess I was taken aback by her preparedness. I had imagined us roaming around without an itinerary, chancing upon cities and monuments—but thank goodness she was so organised. Only a couple of months after we left, Syria descended into a civil war that would alter it in ways we could never have imagined. When we both arrived in Damascus, the Arab Spring was still nascent; the political upheaval set off by the protests in Tunisia was yet to sweep North Africa and the Middle East. That January, all we saw was a country filled with incredible sights and peopled by men and women who, no matter where we went, made us both feel safe and welcome. Syria was, for us, a *coup de foudre*. We loved it from day one.

I had packed a small digital camera and an old analogue Hasselblad. Having forgotten to bring film for the latter, I went out to look for medium-format rolls in Damascus but came back empty-handed. As it turned out, I used my digital camera only sporadically, preferring to write down my perceptions like travellers of old. Returning to those notes, I have been able to reconstruct my cherished memories. I can still see early morning break above the ruins at Palmyra, the cold biting at our ears under pink sky. I remember the eerie silence of the abandoned Byzantine cities close to the Turkish border, the shy and lovable Labrador that lived in our hotel in Aleppo, and the Bedouin family that invited Sandra and I to share tea and bread with them as the sun went down behind ancient sands. I often wonder what became of them, all the kind people we met, people like the guys selling mastic ice cream in the Damascus Bazaar, who, having found out about my Argentinian heritage, asked me incessantly about Maradona and refused to accept my payment.

We saw extraordinary things in Syria, but it was the Syrians who made us fall in love with their beautiful country.

Velyan's House

Words by Oliver Maclennan
Images by Joanna Maclennan

Surrounded by a high stone wall, Velyan's House bathes in the afternoon sun in the old town of Bansko, nestled at the foot of the Pirin mountains in southwest Bulgaria. The courtyard and garden, carpeted with bright yellow leaves, create a picturesque scene. Above the terracotta tiles of the house, a church tower reaches up into the sky. It's hard to believe that danger once lurked in this peaceful place, but between the fourteenth and nineteenth centuries, the Ottoman Empire ruled here with an iron fist.

By the mid-eighteenth century, when Velyan's House was built, the wealthy merchants of Bansko incorporated fortifications into their grand homes. Ivan Hadzhiradonov, one such merchant, spared no expense to ensure his family's safety. Despite bolted gates, escape tunnels, and metal bars on all windows, his precautions proved sadly futile. While on business in Vienna, Ivan's house was ransacked, resulting in the tragic murder of his wife and child.

The house stood empty until the arrival of painter and woodcarver Velyan Ognev. Trained at the Debar School of Art, Veylan had been tasked with renovating the church, and as part of his compensation, he was gifted the house that would later bear his name. Velyan divided the house into two levels: the top for his family and the lower for his work and livestock. Underground passageways, now walled up, once led to the church and the neighbour's house. Upstairs—or via another secret passage at the rear—a sheltered veranda dominated the front, with living quarters behind and at either side.

What sets this property apart are the delicate frescoes adorning the walls inside and the entire exterior. Velyan painted birds and floral motifs on the outside of the house, many in blue, a coveted pigment symbolising purity, tranquillity, and the divine.

Veylan's second wife Sofia was the love of his life. In her bedroom, he painted dreams of a blue-tinged Venice and Istanbul, filled with fantasies of boats, bridges, and soaring towers. One wall features Veylan himself, standing beside a horse, proudly surveying his creation. While Veylan may have doted on her, Sofia, as a wife, was expected to weave. In her workroom, she used a loom, crafting clothes, rugs, and fabrics, some of which can still be found in the second guest room. Here, the frescoes take on a more political tone. A lion weighed down by chains symbolises Bulgaria under Ottoman rule, while opposite, a pair of wolves—representing Velyan and Sofia—carry their cubs to safety. Despite the fears they must have felt, the home emanates warmth and love, evident not only in the frescoes and wood carvings but also in its everyday, domestic details—the heart and soul of every home.

King for a Night

Images by
Miguel Flores-Vianna

When his wife's aunt died in the early '80s, Leonidas Spirthakis knew that their time in New York was up. He and his wife, Panagiota Blachou, had built their lives in Manhattan, working in the restaurant business. Despite their love for the city, it now felt natural and right for them to return home to Hydra to take over Aunt Sofia's taverna and pensione business.

Once they had settled into their new life in the old home, the couple realized that there was little need to make many changes to the business. The recipe was already good it just needed an infusion of their metropolitan flair. As Leonidas explained to me: "We just wanted to make you feel you were king for a night!" They decided to leave their aunt's décor pretty much intact. Sofia had chosen the bright pink and green paints that cover the taverna. On the walls, all the portraits of royalty and politicians stayed put and, in time, the couple added new works by artist clients. On the floor above, the pensione rooms, which had welcomed mostly sponge divers during their Hydra stays in days gone by, also remained the same. Although the old lodgers were gone by then, the rooms with their linens and gently frayed bedspreads were still there, clean and inviting, as though ready for the next check-in.

What did change in the establishment was the atmosphere. Panagiota showed her colors in the kitchen, bringing her brilliance to the dishes, and Leonidas's easy manner and charming smile were soon a success among Hydra's local and visiting clientele. The couple's New York *élan* went a long way during the season and, without much ado, Bill Gates and various English duchesses began calling in to enjoy their hospitality. Everyone who visited was, indeed, made to feel like a king or a queen for the night.

An excerpt from Miguel Flores-Vianna's book:
Haute Bohemians Greece, *Vendome, 2023.*

Outrageous Fortune

Words by Toto Bergamo Rossi
Images by François Halard

The Palazzo Fortuny Museum, formerly Palazzo Pesaro degli Orfei, transports visitors on a journey to the Venice of the first half of the twentieth century, providing a window into its extraordinary artistic and cultural milieu.

The palazzo itself was commissioned in the middle of the fifteenth century, and is one of the finest surviving examples of the Venetian Gothic style. In *The Stones of Venice*, John Ruskin described it as one of the best-conserved works of architecture from the Venetian Quattrocento, free of alterations and additions from subsequent periods. However, in 1898, when the painter, photographer, and designer Mariano Fortuny y Madrazo purchased part of the property, the building, like much of Venice, was in a state of total disrepair. The Republic had fallen to the French a century beforehand, and the city had then found itself under Habsburg rule until 1866. Once the capital of an empire, Venice had been reduced to the status of a province, but it was still a destination for enlightened travellers and artists, who continued to find inspiration in the age-old beauty they saw all around them.

The young Fortuny was welcomed by the city on the lagoon. He came from an artistic Andalusian family: his father was the famous painter and portraitist Mariano Fortuny y Marsal, and his mother Cecilia was the daughter of Federico de Madrazo, the director of the Museo del Prado. He moved from Paris to Venice when he was just eighteen years old, setting up a studio in the large attic of the palazzo. Later, he would purchase the entire building and transform it into his residence, atelier, and workshop alongside Henriette Nigrin, his life-long muse and companion. She was a brilliant stylist, and created many of Fortuny's most iconic dresses here, including the famous Delphos gown, inspired by archaeological excavations at the Sanctuary of Apollo. Soon, Sarah Bernhardt, Eleonora Duse, and Isadora Duncan were sporting Fortuny's designs, and their early success soon reached the United States, where they could count Lillian Gish, Martha Graham, and Ruth St. Denis among their customers.

A few years later, with financing from the industrialist Giovanni Stucky, production began on a range of furnishing fabrics at the new Fabbrica Fortuny on the island of Giudecca. This was an immediate success, confirmed beyond doubt when New York's leading *grande dame*, Consuelo Vanderbilt, chose fabrics produced at Giudecca to decorate her residence.

In 1956 Henriette donated the palazzo and its collections to the municipality of Venice. Today, it offers guests both a vivid impression of the period, and a surfeit of instructive examples in the art of living beautifully.

Wangduechhoeling Palace

Words by Cosmo Brockway
Images by Mark Luscombe-Whyte

In 1862, the first king of Bhutan was born at Wangduechhoeling Palace—a place greatly revered in the Land of the Thunder Dragon. Rising above the fertile rice fields of the Jakar Valley, the palace is a glorious example of Bhutan's architectural vernacular and has long served as a powerful symbol of peace and stability for its people. The palace, or *phodrang*, was the first to be built in Bhutan without a defensive purpose, and its painted facades herald the dawn of the Wangchuk dynasty, which has held the throne since the establishment of the monarchy in 1907.

Largely neglected for the last fifty years, Wangduechhoeling is now undergoing an exciting restoration under the patronage of Queen Mother Tshering Pem Wangchuck. "We are working to restore the palace to its stately beauty while investing in a future that will be a unique showcase for our heritage, craftsmanship, and culture," says Her Majesty, a keen conservationist. Each floor is an homage to the mastery of local carpenters (*zow*) and masons (*dozop*), who were reputed to be so skilful that they could create jewels like this without needing to make a single sketch of their designs beforehand.

One of the triumphs of the restoration has been the use of traditional mineral paints that were used when the palace was first constructed, sensitively applied by specially trained conservation students. Pramod Kumar KG, working on the forthcoming palace museum, notes that "the superb quality of its murals and paintings would have posed a significant challenge at the time of its construction," especially considering that these may have been some of the first expressions of domestic interior art in Bhutan. Inside the enfilades of rooms that line the *shabkor* (four-sided building), the original nineteenth-century colours have been replicated with startling vibrancy: yellow runs riot through the royal chambers, a vivid backdrop to motifs of dancing flowers, auspicious cloud patterns, and abstract animal figures painted in blue, magenta, burnt orange, and green. Even the timber lintels and cornices are gaily decorated, and their once-faded geometric patterns now seem remarkably contemporary.

The future is bright for this storied place. As part of an exciting community outreach program, the palace will host spiritual festivals and archery competitions, and welcome local artisans here to practice traditional crafts like silversmithing, woodturning, and textile weaving. When the new museum opens, Wangduechhoeling will once again tell the story of Bhutan and the Wangchuk dynasty, with objects and treasures carefully chosen for their connection to the stories told to descendants of the courtiers and attendants who served the royal family here in the early 1900s.

The Once and Future Castle

Words by Remy Renzullo
Images by Derry Moore

"That any houses survive at all in private hands is a measure of the resilience of their owners and their sense of trusteeship for the future." So wrote Lord Howard in *The Destruction of the English Country House*, a book published alongside the landmark 1974 V&A exhibition that revitalized the movement to protect Britain's endangered historic buildings. Living by his words, Howard devoted his life to the preservation of the architectural masterpiece that was his also family home. Today, as the steadfast custodians of Castle Howard, his son Nicholas and daughter-in-law Victoria demonstrate that same strength and determination. Their keen eye and vast interest in the decorative arts have made them the perfect partners and clients in our redecoration efforts.

I wanted to create rooms that neither felt brand new, nor frozen in the past. I hoped to convey a certain permanence, a sense of depth and gradual evolution. While little of the previous decoration could be retained, the house's sprawling attics served as a formidable arsenal. On a recent excursion for oil paintings, I found a small study of Charles James Fox, the famous Whig and Howard family friend. It bore a remarkable likeness to the celebrated Holkham portrait by Joshua Reynolds—and there on the back was a scrawled note from Charles Howard, younger son of the 6th Earl of Carlisle, denoting the painter as Reynolds himself! It now hangs in pride of place against the Staffordshire bedroom's hand-dyed apricot silk walls.

I looked to the existing fabric of the house for inspiration. A small dressing room adjacent to the famous Archbishop's bedroom was hung with early 20th century hand-blocked paper in a crosshatch pattern—a perfect backdrop for works on paper. I found a nearly identical version from Mauny, my favorite wallpaper firm, for an East Wing bedroom, where it's a perfect foil to the gilt-framed views of the Bay of Naples, the monumental Victorian brass bed, and the eau-de-nil taffeta curtains that recall the quiet sophistication of a '50s Balmain evening gown.

I'm immensely proud of what we have achieved in this first phase of work on the house. Over the last three years, I have spent more time at Castle Howard than any one other place, but not a day goes by without my being awestruck by its beauty. On a recent visit, we had dinner outside on the East Wing steps, where we watched the sun hang above the North Lake before it receded behind the distant moors. It was a familial moment, modest and human, set against a backdrop of sublime majesty; and therein lies the enduring beauty and magic of this place.

We would like to thank all the homeowners whose homes are included in this book, and all the new and old friends for their support, inspiration, enthusiasm, commitment and belief in *Cabana*.

This book would not have been possible without the generous contributions of:

Anna Abbagnale, Peter Adler, Amy Astley, SJ Axelby, Giovanna Battaglia, Toto Bergamo Rossi, Miorica Bertolotti, Andrew Black, William Blacker, Deeda Blair, Derek Blasberg, Elia Blei, Marco Blei, Francesco Bonami, Francesca Brambilla, Marcantonio Brandolini d'Adda, Coco Brandolini d'Adda, Cosmo Brockway, Pablo Bronstein, Ros Byam Shaw, Oisin Byrne, Violett Caldecott, Santi Caleca, Duncan Campbell, Gregorio Cappa, Laura Capsoni, Fabrizia Caracciolo, Elinore Carmody, Lea Carpenter, Nicolò Castellini Baldissera, Luca Cepparo, Jasper Conran, Suzanne Cooper, Will Cooper, Madison Cox, Antony Crolla, Mark Cropper, Nicholas Cullinan, Vincent Darré, Elisa De Donno, Roberto Delfrati, Matteo De Stefani, Saima Dev, Antonella Di Amario, Alex and Charlotte di Carcaci, Alessandra di Castro, Luke Edward Hall, Ginevra Elkann, Nathalie Farman Farma, Emanuele Farneti, Will Fisher, Miguel Flores-Vianna, Barnaba Fornasetti, Margo Fortuny, Camilla Frances, Natasha A. Fraser, Charlotte Freemantle, Pierre Frey, Goya Gallagher, Martino Gamper, Idarica Gazzoni, Sophie Goodwin, Kath Griffiths, Lena Grivakes, François Halard, Jessica Hayns, Katrin Henkel, Ashley Hicks, Angelica Hicks, India Hicks, Allegra Hicks, Peter Hinwood, Stephan Janson, Teodora Jelic, Ulla Johnson, Debra Kanabis, Ari Kellerman, Patrick Kinmonth, Ömer Koç, Alexis, Nicolas and Laura Kugel, Riccardo Labougle, Raimonda Lanza, Alessandro Laraspata, Aerin Lauder, Nancy Lichterman, Mark Luscombe-Whyte, Lulu Lyte, Joanna and Oliver Maclennan, George Maginis, Fabrizio Malverdi, Marco Mansi, Francesca Mapelli, Federico Marchetti, Alessia Margiotta Broglio, Natalie Massenet, Charlie McCornick, Marian McEvoy, Alessandro Michele, Caterina Mocenni, Antonio Monfreda, Derry Moore, Britt Moran, Carlos Mota, Alessandra Nava, Gianni Nava, Deborah Needleman, David Netto, Duro Olowu, Susana Ordovás, Barbara Orsi Mangelli, Rifat Ozbek, Franco Pagani, Martina Pagani, Umberto Pasti, Roberto Peregalli, Pierpaolo Piccioli, Sara Pierdonà, Filippo Pincolini, Fabrizio Prestinari, Rodman Primack, David Prior, Andrea and Gianluca Reina, Remy Renzullo, Charlotte Rey, Filippo Richeri, Mary Robbins, Markham Roberts, Simone Rossi, Elisa Ruggieri, Emiliano Salci, Lauren Santo Domingo, Felipe Sanguinetti, Laura Sartori Rimini, James Sharp, Eleonora Sicolo, Eugenia Sicolo, Francesca Simpson, Michael Smith, Jim Spivey, Francis Sultana, Giorgio Taroni, Guido Taroni, Virginia Taroni, Mario Tavella, Mario Testino, Michael Trapp, Alessandro and Soledad Twombly, Caio Twombly, Simon Upton, Francesca Urso Ciullo, Bronson Van Wyck, Edouard Vermeulen, Alberta Vianello, Beatrice Vincenzini, Osanna Visconti di Modrone, Stellene Volandes, Diane von Fürstenberg, Tim Walker, Erik Winterstam, Bethan Laura Wood, Brett Wood, Manolo Yllera, Uberta Zambeletti, Roberto Zanetti, Antonia Zanussi, Tino Zervudachi, Sofka Zinovieff.

In memory of Anna Gastel, Manfredi della Gherardesca, Christopher Gibbs, Robert Kime, and Paola Zanussi.

p. 1
Cabana Issue 22 Fall/Winter 2024
PORTFOLIO UZBEKISTAN
Photographs by Miguel Flores-Vianna

p. 28
Cabana Issue 17 Spring/Summer 2022
Cover Fabric by Belmond
A HOUSE OF MAGIC
Photographs by Brett Wood
Excerpt from an article by Susana Ordovás

p. 44
Cabana Issue 19 Spring/Summer 2023
Cover Fabric by Loro Piana
ELECTRIFYING ARCHITECTURE
Photographs by Mark Luscombe-Whyte
Excerpt from an article by Cosmo Brockway

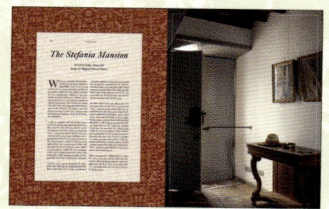

p. 56
Cabana Issue 21 Spring/Summer 2024
THE STEFANIA MANSION
Cover Fabric by Valentino
Photographs by Miguel Flores-Vianna
Excerpt from an article by Sofka Zinovieff

p. 72
Cabana Issue 19 Spring/Summer 2023
Cover Fabric by Loro Piana
INSIDE - OUTSIDE
Photographs by Mark Luscombe-Whyte
Excerpt from an article by Cosmo Brockway

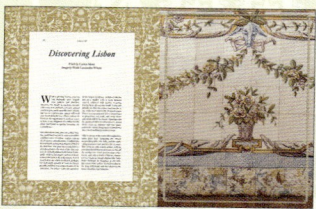

p. 88
Cabana Issue 15 Spring/Summer 2021
Cover Fabric by Ralph Lauren
DISCOVERING LISBON
Photographs by Mark Luscombe-Whyte
Excerpt from an article by Carlos Mota

p. 104
Cabana Issue 17 Spring/Summer 2022
Cover Fabric by Belmond
FINDING TIME
Photographs by François Halard
Excerpt from an article by Nicholas Cullinan

p. 118
Cabana Issue 13 Spring/Summer 2020
Cover Fabric by Roger Vivier
BLESSED BY GODS
Photographs by Miguel Flores-Vianna
Excerpt from an article by Miguel Flores-Vianna

p. 150
Cabana Issue 13 Spring/Summer 2020
Cover Fabric by Roger Vivier
THE STYLISH SUBVERSIONS OF PORTALUPPI
Photographs by Guido Taroni
Excerpt from an article by Nicolò Castellini Baldissera

p. 150
Cabana Issue 18 Fall/Winter 2022
Cover Fabric by Liberty
IN THE PINK
Photographs by Tim Walker
Excerpt from an article by Charlotte di Carcaci

p. 166
Cabana Issue 12 Spring/Summer 2018
Cover Fabric by Fendi
PHARAOHLAND
Photographs by Miguel Flores-Vianna
Excerpt from "Red Porphyry Slab"
by Oliver Hoare

p. 182
Cabana Issue 20 Fall/Winter 2023
Cover Fabric by Tiffany
THE FREEDOM OF CREATIVITY
Photographs by Guido Taroni
Excerpt from an article by Cosmo Brockway

p. 196
Cabana Issue 19 Spring/Summer 2023
Cover Fabric by Loro Piana
THE QUEEN'S HOUSE
Photographs by Miguel Flores-Vianna
Excerpt from an article by Ashley Hicks

p. 208
Cabana Issue 18 Fall/Winter 2022
Cover Fabric by Liberty
TRANSYLVANIA
Photographs by Mark Cropper
Excerpt from an article by William Blacker

p. 226
Cabana Issue 20 Fall/Winter 2023
Cover Fabric by Tiffany
HARMONIOUS SIMPLICITY
Photographs by Miguel Flores-Vianna
Excerpt from an article by Natasha A. Fraser

p. 238
Cabana Issue 14 Fall/Winter 2020
Cover Fabric by Clarence House
AN UNEQUALLED ARCHITECTURE
Photographs by Mark Luscombe-Whyte
Excerpt from an article by Anuradha S. Naik

p. 254
Cabana Issue 18 Fall/Winter 2022
Cover Fabric by Liberty
THE VIEW FROM VISTORTA
Photographs by Miguel Flores-Vianna
Excerpt from an article by Natasha A. Fraser

p. 270
Cabana Issue 21 Spring/Summer 2024
Cover Fabric by Valentino
WYETHS' WORLD
Photographs by Ari Kellerman
Excerpt from an article by Remy Renzullo

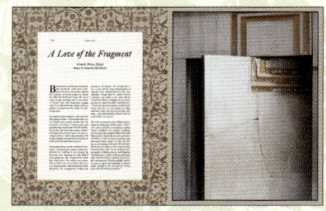

p. 286
Cabana Issue 19 Spring/Summer 2023
Cover Fabric by Loro Piana
A LOVE OF THE FRAGMENT
Photographs by **Antonio Monfreda**
Excerpt from an article by **Marco Mansi**

p. 302
Cabana Issue 15 Spring/Summer 2021
Cover Fabric by Ralph Lauren
THE PROMENADE OF DONNA ENRICHETTA
Photographs by **Guido Taroni**
Excerpt from an article by **Umberto Pasti**

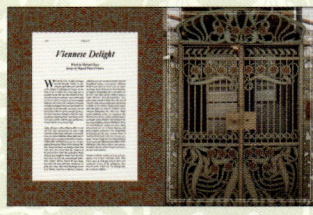

p. 318
Cabana Issue 10 Fall/Winter 2018
Cover Fabric by Dries Van Noten
VIENNESE DELIGHT
Photographs by **Miguel Flores-Vianna**
Excerpt from an article by **Michael Huey**

p. 334
Cabana Issue 15 Spring/Summer 2021
Cover Fabric by Ralph Lauren
IN THE MIND'S EYE
Photographs by **Miguel Flores-Vianna**
Excerpt from an article by **Miguel Flores-Vianna**

p. 352
Cabana Issue 19 Spring/Summer 2023
Cover Fabric by Loro Piana
VELYAN'S HOUSE
Photographs by **Joanna Maclennan**
Excerpt from an article by **Oliver Maclennan**

p. 366
Cabana Issue 19 Spring/Summer 2023
Cover Fabric by Loro Piana
KING FOR A NIGHT
Photographs by **Miguel Flores-Vianna**
Excerpt from Haute Bohemians Greece
by Miguel Flores-Vianna

p. 374
Cabana Issue 21 Spring/Summer 2024
Cover Fabric by Valentino
OUTRAGEOUS FORTUNE
Photographs by **François Halard**
Excerpt from an article by **Toto Bergamo Rossi**

p. 390
Cabana Issue 21 Spring/Summer 2024
Cover Fabric by Valentino
WANGDUECHHOELING PALACE
Photographs by **Mark Luscombe-Whyte**
Excerpt from an article by **Cosmo Brockway**

p. 402
Cabana Issue 20 Fall/Winter 2023
Cover Fabric by Tiffany
THE ONCE AND FUTURE CASTLE
Photographs by **Derry Moore**
Excerpt from an article by **Remy Renzullo**

insert

Cabana Issue 19 Spring/Summer 2023
UMBERTO PASTI:
MY WAYS
Photographs by **Guido Taroni,**
Ngoc Minh Ngo, Mattia Balsamini
Article by Marian McEvoy

insert

CABANA COVERS
Photographs by Filippo Pincolini

CABANA ANTHOLOGY: The Anniversary Edition
First published in 2024 by The Vendome Press
Vendome is a registered trademark of The Vendome Press LLC

VENDOME PRESS US
PO Box 566
Palm Beach, FL 33480

VENDOME PRESS UK
Worlds End Studios
132–134 Lots Road
London, SW10 0RJ

www.vendomepress.com

Copyright © 2024 The Vendome Press LLC and Cabana Magazine LTD

Images
© 2018, 2019, 2020, 2021, 2022, 2023, 2024 Miguel Flores-Vianna: pp. 1–15, 57–71, 119–133, 167–181, 197–207, 227–237, 255–269, 319–351, 367–373
© 2020, 2021, 2023, 2024 Mark Luscombe-Whyte: pp. 45–55, 73–103, 238–253, 391–401
© 2020, 2021, 2023 Guido Taroni: pp. 135–149, 183–195, 303–317
© 2022 Brett Wood: pp. 29–43
© 2023 Derry Moore: pp. 403–421
© 2022, 2024 Francois Halard: pp. 105–117, 375–389
© 2022 Tim Walker: pp. 151–164
© 2024 Ari Kellerman: pp. 271–285
© 2021 Antonio Monfreda: pp. 287–301
© 2023 Joanna Maclennan: pp. 353–365
© 2023 Mark Cropper: pp. 209–225
"Umberto Pasti: My Ways" insert: images © 2023 Guido Taroni, Mattia Balsamini, Ngoc Minh Ngo.
"Cabana Covers" insert: images © 2024 Filippo Pincolini.
Copyright for each text is held by its respective author.

All rights reserved. No part of the contents of this book may be reproduced
in whole or in part without prior written permission from the publisher.

Distributed worldwide by Abrams Books

ISBN 978-0-86565-451-8

For Vendome Press
Beatrice Vincenzini, Mark Magowan, and Francesco Venturi, *Publishers*
Jim Spivey, *Production Director*

For Cabana Magazine
Martina Mondadori, *Editor-in-Chief*
Christoph Radl, *Creative Director*
Barbara Spinelli, *Editorial Director*
Giulia Biscottini, *Graphic Designer*

Library of Congress Cataloging-in-Publication Data available upon request.

Printed and bound in China by 1010 Printing International Ltd.
First Printing